SMALL SEA CREATURES

THE SEA

Jason Cooper

The Rourke Corporation, Inc.
Vero Beach, Florida 32964

Edited by Sandra A. Robinson

PHOTO CREDITS
© James H. Carmichael: cover, pages 17 and 21; © Mary A. Cote: page 18; © James P. Rowan: page 12; © Lynn M. Stone: title page, pages 4, 7, 8, 10, 13, 15

LIBRARY OF CONGRESS
Library of Congress Cataloging-in-Publication Data
Cooper, Jason, 1942-
 Small sea creatures / by Jason Cooper.
  p. cm. — (Discovery library of the sea)
 Includes index.
 Summary: Describes such marine animals as shrimp, horseshoe crabs, starfish, mollusks, and sponges.
  ISBN 0-86593-230-1
  1. Marine invertebrates—Juvenile literature. 2. Marine fauna—Juvenile literature. [1. Marine animals. 2. Invertebrates.] I. Title. II. Series: Cooper, Jason, 1942-   Discovery library of the sea.
 QL122.2.C66 1992
 592.092—dc20   92-16073
                                                      CIP
                                                      AC

Printed in the USA

TABLE OF CONTENTS

SMALL SEA CREATURES

Walking along the seashore after a storm is exciting. Each step brings a new discovery—sponge, jellyfish, snail, crab, coral rock and dozens of animals that only a **marine biologist** (one who studies sea creatures) would know.

By seeing what the storm waves have tossed ashore, one can see some of what lives in the sea!

The oceans are homes for thousands of **species,** or kinds, of little animals. Most are soft and boneless, although many marine animals do have shells.

Discovering a sand dollar, washed onto a Florida shore

CRUSTY CREATURES

Some of the best-known and best-tasting marine animals have a hard, crusty surface. These are **crustaceans** such as crabs, lobsters, shrimp and krill.

Crustaceans, along with some other small sea animals, can lose a leg or claw and grow a new one in its place.

A crustacean's shell does not become larger as the animal inside it grows. Every so often a crustacean has to shed its out-grown shell and produce a larger one.

The Maine lobster,
a seafood lover's delight

HORSESHOE CRABS

Horseshoe crabs are not "true" crabs. Although they do have a hard shell, they have neither the claws nor shape of other crabs.

Horseshoe crabs are easy to identify. They have a horseshoe's shape and a long, sharp tail.

Horseshoe crabs are common along the Atlantic coast. Thousands of them crawl ashore each spring to lay eggs in the loose, wet sand.

Horseshoe crabs prowl
the Atlantic beaches

SEA STARS AND CUCUMBERS

Sea stars, or starfish, are named for their star shape.

Starfish have five or more arms that they use to open the shells of the clams and snails they eat. If a starfish loses an arm, another will grow in its place.

Sea cucumbers look like big, warty pickles. Like their starfish cousins, sea cucumbers move along the ocean bottom on tiny, tubelike feet.

An ochre sea star (starfish) clings to rock on an Oregon seashore

One of the strangest fish—the seahorse

The blue crab, a common crustacean of the Atlantic

SEA URCHINS AND DOLLARS

Two more curious relatives of starfish are sea urchins and sand dollars.

Sea urchins look like pincushions because of their long, pointed spines. Sea urchins feed on marine plants. The spines protect them from most **predators,** or hunting animals.

Sand dollars are really just a different form of sea urchin. Unlike the ball-shaped urchins, sand dollars are flat, like silver dollars. And instead of spines, sand dollars have a fringe of little bristles.

Some short-spined sea urchins can be held—carefully!

MOLLUSKS

Perhaps the best-known sea animals of all are **mollusks**—snails, clams and their cousins.

Most mollusks are protected by a shell, or shells. Sea snails have a single shell. Clams and oysters, however, have a pair of matching shells that clamp together.

Squids, octopuses, sea slugs and sea hares are common mollusks without outside shells. They protect themselves in other ways. The sea hare releases a nasty purple dye.

The octopus is a mollusk without the protection of a shell

SPONGES

Don't confuse the sponge in a kitchen with a living sponge, which is one of the sea's most simple animals.

Sponges live by filtering tiny **organisms,** or living things, from water that passes through them.

Sponges grow in a remarkable number of shapes and sizes. They may be shaped like bowls, fingers, baseballs and other objects.

Most sponges are fairly small, but this barrel sponge is an exception

JELLYFISH

Jellyfish, like starfish, are not fish at all. They are basically floating blobs filled with a jellylike substance. Jellyfish move by pumping their bodies back and forth.

Like their relatives, corals and sea anemones, jellyfish wear a fringe of stinging **tentacles.**

The tentacles look like a ring of tiny fingers or long strings. The tentacles' poison kills the small animals that jellyfish eat.

Jellyfish tentacles can give people painful wounds.

A jellyfish afloat in a warm sea

LITTLE FISH

Many kinds of little fish live in the ocean. They are important food for larger sea animals.

One of the strangest fish in the sea is the little seahorse, which grows no larger than eight inches. It swims upright, and it certainly doesn't look like a fish.

The female seahorse drops her eggs into a pouch on the male seahorse. The eggs remain there until they hatch.

Glossary

crustacean (krus TAY shun) — a group of small, shelled creatures with bodies in attached sections; for example, lobsters, shrimp, crabs, barnacles

marine biologist (muh REEN bi AHL uh jist) — one who studies living things of the ocean

mollusk (MAHL usk) — a group of soft, boneless animals usually protected by hard shells of their own making; for example, clams, oysters, snails

organism (OR gan izm) — a living thing

predator (PRED uh tor) — an animal that kills other animals for food

species (SPEE sheez) — within a group of closely related animals, such as sea anemones, one certain kind or type (*green* sea anemone)

tentacles (TEN tah kulz) — a group of long, flexible body parts usually growing around an animal's mouth and used for touching, grasping or stinging

23

INDEX